Thoughts At Midnight

-R.E. ALBERS-

Thoughts At Midnight

ReadersMagnet, LLC

Thoughts At Midnight
Copyright © 2020 by R.E. Albers

Published in the United States of America
ISBN Paperback: 978-1-951775-19-3
ISBN Hardback: 978-1-951775-59-9
ISBN eBook: 978-1-951775-20-9

All rights reserved. No part of this publication may be reproduced, stored in a retrieval system or transmitted in any way by any means, electronic, mechanical, photocopy, recording or otherwise without the prior permission of the author except as provided by USA copyright law.

The opinions expressed by the author are not necessarily those of ReadersMagnet, LLC.

ReadersMagnet, LLC
10620 Treena Street, Suite 230 | San Diego, California, 92131 USA
1.619.354.2643 | www.readersmagnet.com

Book design copyright © 2020 by ReadersMagnet, LLC. All rights reserved.
Cover design by Ericka Obando
Interior design by Shemaryl Tampus

1. Thoughts at Midnight

My soul it longs to soar.
These earth-bound chains
To cast aside.
Below these sparkling stars
I can but dream of You,
But ah, above
I'm called to go.

2. Wonderment

The woods are hushed and still,
A silence undisturbed by the falling snow.
These delicate fragments
I capture in my hand.
In their microscopic world,
Exquisite beauty
Is so fleeting.
And one by one they melt away,
And I will never see another the same.

3. Phantasy

Like the music of the soul
The bursting sweet inside
An ache that pines
For what has been lost, yet never found.
Like fairies dancing in the sun

A common world has not,
Eyes to see, nor hearts to feel
The beauty of a fading fantasy.

4. Reflection

I wonder what held him there.
When in his palm the entire expanse
Of creation was laid-
Just specks of dust crying out his name.
When flaming swords awaited his command,
I wonder what stayed his hand.

I wonder why he never uttered his defense.
When every captor was his captive,
The highest king his lowest subject-
Their poverty poured out on an angry crowd.
When his breath formed their very souls,
I wonder why he shut his mouth.

He chose instead to die as the thieves
His cross stood between.
He chose the scourge, the blood, the shame-
While even his father turned away.

5. Decay

There's something unsettling
About decay.
How every civilization builds
Upon the bones
Of all the ones before.
How death will touch us all
With withered hands,
And reminds us by the passing time
That we were never meant to stay.

6. Mortality and the Soul

Though I wander far alone
I cannot see what others see.
This I sense is not my home,
And I am not as free.
I only live between the space
Of thoughts of heaven
And reality.

But there will yet come a time
When I shall leave this place,

And no more shrink to cross the line
Between this mold of earth
And eternity.

7. Rains

I am bound to the song
Of the wind and rain
On the green green earth
At first glimpse of spring.

8. The Deep White Nothing

I can't let go.
Though I cannot breathe.
The water is dark and clear,
And I slip out from view.
Sweet release.
The stars above burn out and fall-
Raining down like snow.
And it's cold, this emptiness I feel,
Where your hand touches mine,
And you let go.

9. For John, Henry, Charlotte, and Percy

She sleeps beneath the ancient oak
Who stands forgotten
Where the sweetgrass grows.

And I wonder if they even know
How long its been since that summer snow?
How many footsteps passed by
That faded out and came to stay
Or trembled at the whispers
Of the ones who knelt to pray?
And here at twilight
Perhaps, did I perceive,
You weeping for your children
Amid the murmur of the trees?

10. Legends

I wish I knew
Why the willow sighed-
Did he miss those fairy folk
Who used to tend his
Quietness?
Or did they visit him perhaps
Long before this present
Loneliness?

11. Loneliness

She wears her pain like a cloak.
Hiding beneath the secrets
That whisper round her feet.
She sleeps in the quiet shadows
Taking comfort in the solace

That only suffering brings.
She removes her mask in the darkness
Laying it aside like armor
Until the dawn has come again.

12. Stolen

You stole away my light.
The wind loves it when it plays-
Ever chasing that ethereal delight,
Dancing into happier days.
Yet with all your charm,
Pleasure came only to harm.
And that curtain closed I do not doubt-
One woeful night
Your breath blew it out.

13.

I didn't come, I wasn't there.
You didn't see me, you didn't care.
Such simple words but,
Maybe it's too complex
When we're looking for a meaning
That was never there.

14. Temptation's Ruse

When temptation rose before me
In all its glittery golden hues,
I caught a glimpse
Of all the charred and ruined souls
That hide behind the curtain
Of temptation's ruse.
And I couldn't escape the vision
So I closed my eyes,
But their corrupted state
Was etched into my mind.

15. These are the Days

These are the days I love so well.
Rain-filtered drops of jeweled sun
Touched by mornings verdant spell.
Follow me down to the sunset shore
Through the forest's whispery roar
Stealing away from all that isn't true,
Evening stars in a turquoise blue,
And every moment I spend with you.

16. Brevity

Life is but a temporary silvered thing
He flies at dusk on sorrowed wing-
Comes and goes without a word,
Or traces of its leaving.

17. Morning

The heavens lower
Betwixt the earth and I
Rendering her proportionate view
Of lonely sorrows past,
And present mercies new.

18. Memories

Maybe I have dwelt too long
Existing in the past.
Maybe I have dreamed too oft
Of the magic spell you cast.
Recklessly resisted you, white dove.
In clouded orb of hazy shades,
Ever changing you, my changeless love-
Some shadowed shape that only fades.

19. For an Old Friend

Won't you walk with me a mile?
We haven't spoke for quite a while.
If only for that solemn sight,
Softly woke in ebony night-
Still remembered when we went.
And here again we're rent-
The link not stayed, nor to yield is prone
Because of where we strayed alone.

20. Selfishness

Is there for joy a cage?
My self-entitled will
Unable still
To reach beyond my rage?
My beating heart
Has loved the part
Unyielded pride allowed.
This world I've owned,
And grace disowned
Though God my lips avowed.

Despair I've found
No reason sound
It thrives upon my set of mind.
Unhappiness-
In pleasure, this
The loss of it I've pined.

And all for guilt
Unrepentance built-
In vain I strove to win.
The self-made sin
A prison then
No joy could enter in.
And yet for me
On cursed tree,
My God, my Savior gave
Of His own will

For others still
His life for theirs to save.

How wretched then
That I rebel again
When I dear Christ forsake,
And so should I
My self deny-
Be crucified for others sake.

21. Money

Men have chased it.
Generations have hoarded it.
Crowned kings
Their cruel reigns
Have claimed
Ill-gotten gains
From blood and toil-
The backs of poorer men
Have maimed.

And all for what?
Death soon will steal from them
Their tarnished glory…
And the gates of heaven shut.

22. The Poet

Her soul is made of cold autumn nights-
She wanders amid the stars,
And breathes into a quiet world
What only fancy knows,
And perhaps a meteorite
On which her thoughts alight.

It's on these wings she alone can fly-
And who's to say it's just a dream,
This universe of her making?
She's left the moon to die,
She's passed a whole galaxy by.
"I'll not return," says she,
"I'll not cease to burn
Until the entirety
Of that distant sparkling sky
Is less bright a fire than I."

But the match is no match for the flame,
And she has no natural wit for the game-
She who would not be a pawn.
And parted with imagined feathers,
She sinks once more to rising dawn,
Caught up by earthly tethers.

23. September Equinox

Quiet sorrow gathers
With the shadows
At the close of summer's light.
The stars of evening
Listen solemn while I pray.
All that's broken,
All that's lost
These tears will wash away.
And as the leaves shall surely die
With the fall of Autumn's crisp dark night,
This my heart
Shall turn to ashen gray.

24. To the Wind

There is something in the nature
Of the wild, free wind
On a chilly Autumn day.
Across the hills capped with green,
And hues of color yet unseen,
Under clouds of lowered rain
Creates a misty world again.
And I do not know why
When I hear its wailing cry-
I do not know why,
It creeps inside this cozy room
And pulls my feet away.

25. Carpe Noctem

I cannot "seize the night."
I cannot hold it fast,
Or dream that it will last.
There is no will or might
Could a little time persuade
To change the course it's made.
Nor ever more a lovely light
Than in your radiance cast,
Pale empress dressed in white.

Soft whispering trees,
Oh, did you speak of her?
Say has she come to stay?
Has she come to gaze
Upon the Autumn leaves?

26. I will never be a damask rose.

Those cool gloved fingers,
They've never met the sun-
I'll never strike a painted pose.

I can't be bought with rings.
Those promised gifts,
They cannot satisfy-
I've little care for useless things.

You, if ever a tale have told
Of longing for a soul-
You have bought but grief,
And sold your love for gold.

27. For a Stranger

They stole your dreams
While you were young,
And plundered, laid a waste.
For they cannot see your beauty
With their unobserving eyes.
But spirit they could not take,
Nor of mind a captive make
For you are smiling still-
And you do not believe their lies.

28. The Pianist

A finite scale I find,
But endless possibility.
I dare not sound a key,
For I've a finite mind.

29. Blue Veil

You hide a self within yourself
And how carefully you mask it.
Let them wonder at your coldness,

Let them dare to ask it.
But you must convince them of your bitterness,
So you trade emotion
For an emptiness,
And so a golden sunlit room
For a silent porcelain tomb.
A little part of you
For a shadow,
And a veil of blue.

30. In the Mirror

And you, who are you?
Glass eyes that mimic me,
What secrets do you know?
Lost eyes, I ask of thee,
What is it that I'm looking for?
Answers elude me-
It isn't constant anymore.

31. Oddity

Black and white ideas
In a world of grays.
A novelty of contradictions
In a single word on the page.

32. Self-portrait

You, at home with yourself,
And yet alone
In the company
Of an entire world.

33. I spent a night with Sorrow.

She sought to comfort me.

34. Pride

The proudest man
The man who boasts
Of righteousness.
He has perhaps forgot
The work of God
Is done with quietness.

35. You have I loved as the stars

That burn at night.
Eclipsed by the sun
That rules the day
But ever present,
Still ablaze-
Though out of sight.

36. My heart, muted, prays

That things I loved once,
Would suffice for a night
Or two.

37. Moonrise

At every moonrise
There's a hollow feeling,
A little despairing,
Lonely torment
In the quietness of night's descent.
For the solemn thought,
A little sorrow-
That time unnoticed passed-
That faces, beloved,
May be gone tomorrow.

38. To love-

Memorial.
I leave but a paltry
Remnant of a heart
In thy sacrificial grave.
Ah, I feel the death of thee-
A love that was not,
Nor ever more hence
Shall be.

39. Deep still blue

Washing over my head,
Lost in view,
I hear Your quiet tread.
You who spoke
And colored fathoms
Untainted by soil
Or human design.
Of all creation,
This I love most of thine.

40. Pajaros (Birds)

Captive am I,
Yet if I were free-
Contentment
To stay with thee.
For there is no
Imprisonment
Such as loneliness,
Nor happiness
As in thy company.

41. Nightmares

The night was blue,
The stars were dim
For want of Him.

A full moon rose,
A wintery bright
O'er earth as black as white.
No color hued
That spectrum sight,
Nor sound atoned
For silence quite.

As knife to blood,
The chill of fear-
A shadow doth appear
Glimmering in the light.
It was a stranger,
A face I knew,
Once better than you-
That is, it was my own.

42. For them that dream in solitude

Of bold adventure-
To dare perhaps they would
If they understood.
It takes a quiet soul
To stand undaunted-
That in them sleeps
A greater valiancy
Than all the tongues
That merely boast of bravery.

43. Love is a gift.

Not a prize
That it can be won
Or bought.
No, 'tis free,
Yet not cheaply given-
Asking nothing for itself,
But that it might go on
Giving.

44. I want to be as part of the earth as a tree.

As glorious as the entrance of the sun
On the stage of dawn
When it has first begun.
As secret as a moonlit sea-
What creatures lie beneath,
I may never see.
And if I were a bird,
I'd fly as high and free,
But I am nothing but myself,
And so I'll just be me.

45. Pictures cannot suffice.

Simple words are these-
This burning heart
For nature's art
No portrait could appease.

R.E. Albers

The sapphire sky-
That jeweled heaven,
The taste of Autumn
In the twilight air.
No, 'tis not enough to view it-
I must become it-
Else it's beauty
Should be lost on me.

46. White Stag

Listen, can you hear them?
The hounds and the horsemen
Riding down the trail?
The bugles sounding clear,
Ringing through the vale.
The light is breaking in the woods,
And the sun is shining fair-
The cantering of horse's hooves
Singing in the air.

They come to claim your coat
As soft as fresh spun snow.
They come a-hunting with the bow.
Swiftly, fly- onward go-
You should not a trophy fall,
To hang debased in a marble hall.
For wild thou art,
And wild you shall remain.

47. Set to Self-Destruct

Where did you go-
You with the dreamer eyes?
The light they've held
Have captivated skies-
It's turned to lies.
And how did you fall?
You watched the smiles of friends
All turn to scorn.
Your lovely wings
Are ripped and torn.
When did you know-
Midst the countless others,
Perhaps you were forgot?
You grew jealous,
You weren't what they thought.

Who made you
Captive of the thief of dreams?
Who turned your
Visions into sighs?
But it's not who it seems,
This thief of dreams.

48. Haven't I shed enough tears

To water other souls?

49. Somehow,

Someday,
Someone-
Such a one
As you.

50. My love for you

I cannot change.
And so my heart
It breaks in rhymes,
And stains in blue.

51. To love thee, Christ,

Is to bear thy suffering,
And make it mine.
To follow thee,
Is thy cross preferring,
My willful heart despise,
And make it thine.

52. Is there any other beauty

Than the holiness of God?
All the glory of creation
He painted with His blessing.
In each us, an unfilled part,

A longing for the purest art,
A mirror of His heart.

53. I keep discovering shards of myself

That I once dedicated
To you.

54. Pain, what a thief it is!

Theft of body, parasite of sense,
Poison to the frail heartbeat-
Cherished dreams discarded.
All is clouded,
All is shrouded-
Reeks of pain's perfume.
And trapped within that fog,
Resides that one residual thing
Unwearied, still untainted-
Spirit from its mad tortures
Yet is free.

55. The heart says "Yes."

The head cautions, "Slow."
Will you too say, "No"?

56. Rain comes softly

And so do you.
Catch me quick because I'm falling
Through the clouds that are
Your eyes.

57. There is a pain in existence

In the twilight shades of life,
As it awaits the certainty of night.
Our souls alight with esp`erance of death.

58. Where are you

Under the diamond canopy tonight?
As the moon
Bent her face in the evening light
Autumn tried to whisper your name,
And reminded me you never came.

I wish I
Could miss you and go back to sleep.
But I know
I promised you, and promises I keep.
I'm still waiting under the willow tree,
And Winter, she comes to stay with me.
And you've been gone
For seven summers long.

59. Winter Anthem

Faded are the summer lilies,
Crystallized in death they lay-
Petals folded and gray.

Winds of winter whispering round me,
Casts a shadow with the snow.
Wish that I could lock away this tempest-
I cannot change it though.

60. There is a sense.

When you are here-
A kind of pressure,
A swelling, sweeping feeling
In the heart
That makes the pulses dance.
Buoyant, rooted, riveted, solid,
Strong, softened,
Brilliant, comforting, firm, forgiving-
Of these things in your presence I am certain-
Absence from pain.

61. We fall in love by degrees.

At first by smiles,
A mere trinket
Transfixion of the eyes.
And then the edges of the heart,

And then its diamond core,
And then, by small expansion-
The soul.

62. Truth was a fragile thing

You shattered
On the quiet constancy
Of your marbled lies.

63. January Sky

I watched you dancing,
Laughing in the sun.
Clouds they slip away,
Lazy summer days-
Tell me, where have they gone?

In mist and starlight
Moonbeams in your eyes.
I thought I saw you here,
It wasn't crystal clear-
Tell me, where have you gone?

All silver rainbows
In a dark gray sky.
My spirit crying,
I thought I saw you flying—
Tell me, when can I come?

I wish you were here tonight-
I've been missing you.
I wish I may, I wish I might-
Do you miss me too?
I'm wishing I could be with you
Under my January sky.

64. I'm drifting out,

Drowning quietly-
In these oceans of regret,
I still remember
You.

65. Oh, there's much I could've been,

But I cannot be what I was then.
For love and other things,
These all have passed return of Spring-
As well as you.

66. Life is a tale of tragedies

All ill-fitting silences,
And glances that speak too much,
Yet say too little.

67. That Next Place

I want to stand where the wind is free,
And behold the edge of the heavens-
Far above this
Temporary majesty.

www.ingramcontent.com/pod-product-compliance
Lightning Source LLC
LaVergne TN
LVHW040203080526
838202LV00042B/3309